"Many people aspire to be leaders. Few truly understand that the foundational bedrock of the privilege of leadership in the kingdom of God is servanthood. You will find *Serving with Honor* to be one of the clearest expositions of what leadership in the church is to be. It is written by Steve Dixon, who is, of all the leaders I know, probably the most qualified on the planet to do so. This work provides a real-life model of leadership along with Steve's invaluable insights from his personal journey. I highly recommend this read to all who aspire to leadership roles in the house of the Lord!"

Alan Platt
Leader and Founder of Doxa Deo Ministries
Pretoria, South Africa

"The Kingdom of God is a backward kingdom. To go up you have to go down. To be first you have to be last. And to be the greatest you have to be the servant. Steve Dixon is a friend and pastor who has walked and lived this book by example. *Serving with Honor* will not only teach you the heart and characteristics of a true servant, but it will also help you to impart that spirit to the next generation."

Terry Nance
Author of *God's Armor Bearer*
Pastor of Impact Church
Sherwood, Arkansas

"These are outstanding insights into the powerful principle of servant leadership, which, according to Jesus, is the key to effective ministry in his kingdom. The message of this book goes beyond mere intellectual comprehension and speaks to the heart from which genuine servanthood must flow. More important than touching on leadership, *Serving with Honor* focuses on why and how to lead with honor. Steve has provided a powerful handbook for those of us who want to become better leaders. His book is a must-read for "next generation" leaders! Its blend of biblical teaching and practical application is both inspiring and refreshing."

Kemp Holden
Founding Pastor of Harvest Time Church
Chairman of Worldwide Evangelism
Fort Smith, Arkansas

"There is no greater joy in life than seeing authentic servanthood in action. Steve (my son) has captured the essence of leadership in *Serving with Honor*. I have enjoyed observing Steve teach these principles in order to release individuals to discover and fulfill their God-given destinies. Read this book, learn to live it, and watch what God does. As Steve says, 'God has already done the heavy lifting. Now he is asking us to simply follow his instructions.' Enjoy!"

C.L. "Red" Dixon
Founding Co-Pastor of Christian Life Cathedral
Fayetteville, Arkansas

SERVING WITH HONOR

Walking in the Way of Jesus

Pastor Steve Dixon

Serving with Honor: Walking in the Way of Jesus
Steve Dixon

70X7 Publishing
Fayetteville, AR

Library of Congress Control Number: 2016904906

Printed in the United States of America

ISBN #978-1-944187-05-7

Dedication

To the love of my life, my wife Eva Cosette (Cozy) Dixon. You are my constant source of inspiration and encouragement. I am forever indebted to you. I Love you dearly!

Acknowledgments

Special thanks to Bobby Howard, Sue Whitely, and Linda Apple for gracing me through this project. Thank you for helping make my words readable and sensible.

The foundation of ministry is character.

The nature of ministry is service.

The motive for ministry is love.

The measure of ministry is sacrifice.

The authority of ministry is submission.

The purpose of ministry is the glory of God.

The tools of ministry are the Word of God
and prayer.

The privilege of ministry is growth.

The power of ministry is the Holy Spirit,

and the model for ministry is Jesus Christ.

—Warren W. Wiersbe and David W. Wiersbe

A Note from the Author

It is my firm conviction that God gave each of us gifts when he created us. It is our responsibility and joy to develop those gifts to be used as tools that will bring success and happiness to ourselves and, more importantly, to those God brings to us to mentor and impart the wisdom we have gained.

Growing up in a ministry family, I had deeply significant spiritual relationships early on in life. My father is a great man and successful pastor who was part of a larger network of pastors. And there was no shortage of other ministry models in my life. As a young person, I saw the fundamentals of the Christian faith lived out in real life by those who continue to shape my life and ministry to this day. I consider myself blessed because of this.

I was taught young to serve and give. I learned to value the fruit and gifts of the Holy Spirit, and I learned to value the precious fellowship of other believers. All of these things allowed me to start my life of serving in full-time ministry miles ahead of where I would have otherwise. I am grateful to my father and the men and women who mentored me at the beginning of my ministry.

It is in that spirit of gratitude that I write these thoughts. I hope some of my experiences will help you as you make your life journey with Christ in whatever pillar of society your gifts and talents open to you.

Throughout my forty-plus years of ministry, I have observed many men and women succeed and fail. It is my observation that many of the heartbreaking stories I have heard stem from a lack of discipline in the areas I cover in the following pages. In them I offer my thoughts on the topic of *serving with honor*, drawn from the rich variety of perspectives that have influenced my life. I also share some of my own personal strengths and challenges. I am convinced that honor builds our lives and ministries.

I certainly do not consider myself the shining example of what an honoring servant of God should look like. But I do believe a great God has blessed my attempts to serve him with honor, and that he is gracing my life and my ministry with his favor. I pray that some of what I have learned will help you.

I have attempted to offer practical thoughts concerning spiritual truths, hoping all who read it will be able to use some part of it. Intentional obedience to the precepts and principles of the holy Scriptures brings honor to God. And as we offer honor to others, honor from God himself becomes our reward.

I pray this book will bless you. We are all on this journey together, as we share our hard-earned knowledge with one another along the way. I hope you are blessed by these words, and I hope you will find truths here that you can share with other sojourners.

Serve well,

Steve Dixon
Senior Pastor, *Christian Life Cathedral*
Fayetteville, Arkansas, USA

Contents

Introduction

When we choose to follow Christ and become students of the Word of God, we see there is one fundamental truth in Christ's teachings and in the way he humbly lived his life: Christ came to *serve*—to be the servant of all.

Christ modeled for all of us a life of service and sacrifice: *"For even the Son of Man came not to be served but to serve others and to give his life as a ransom for many"* (Mark 10:45, NLT).

Christ lovingly served all of humanity, even to the point of sacrificing his very life on the cross. He then gave the Holy Spirit to all believers so that we could fulfill the desire of the Father, serving as Christ served and loving as Christ loved. May we always be mindful of the fact that the one who calls us to serve is the same one who enables us to serve in the power of the Holy Spirit. He is also the one who has given us distinct gifts so that we can serve faithfully and effectively.

Our serving may be somewhat sacrificial in different seasons, but just remember the prophet's words to the king: *"Obedience is better than sacrifice."* We need to remind ourselves of this often. That familiar quote is from 1 Samuel 15:22 (NLT), where the prophet, Samuel, rebuked Israel's first king, Saul, for not remaining obedient to the instruction of the Lord. Here is the rest of the passage: *"But Samuel replied, 'What is more*

*pleasing to the Lord: your burnt offerings and sacri-
fices or your obedience to his voice? Listen! Obedience
is better than sacrifice, and submission is better than
offering the fat of rams. Rebellion is as sinful as witch-
craft, and stubbornness as bad as worshiping idols. So
because you have rejected the command of the Lord, he
has rejected you as king' "* (1 Samuel 15:22-23 (NLT).

In following the life and times of King Saul, we discover that his story serves as the dramatic backdrop
for Israel's next king: God's man, David. David's story
is rich and filled with divine purpose, for David would
prophetically establish the throne of the coming Mes-
siah, Jesus Christ.

There is great significance placed on the biblical
narrative of David's character, his conduct, and the
consequences of his decisions in life. He was chosen
and anointed by God to be king in spite of his humanness. In fact, the prophet Samuel sought David out
and anointed him to be king of Israel long before he sat
on the throne. The life of David is truly inspiring and
filled with good instruction on how to *serve with honor.*

Servanthood is the philosophical foundation of
the kingdom of God. *"He (Jesus) sat down, called the
twelve disciples over to him, and said, 'Whoever wants
to be first must take last place and be the servant of
everyone else' "* (Mark 9:35, NLT, parentheses added).

**"Servanthood is the philosophical foundation
of the kingdom of God."**

What a privilege it is to participate in the greatest
cause that man has ever known: the advancement

of the kingdom of God in the earth! May we humbly submit our lives to the service of Christ and faithfully steward our gifts and talents so that his will may be accomplished through our lives. *"My help and glory are in God—granite-strength and safe-harbor-God—So trust him absolutely, people; lay your lives on the line for him. God is a safe place to be"* (Psalm 62:7, MSG).

Christ has invited us to be his disciples, which means we can be students of his teaching and examples of his love, grace, and wisdom to our world. *"Jesus said to the people who believed in him, 'You are truly my disciples if you remain faithful to my teachings. And you will know the truth, and the truth will set you free' "* (John 8:31-32, NLT).

Discipleship is a lifelong journey of becoming like Jesus. It is important to understand that while salvation is instantaneous, discipleship occurs progressively as one follows Christ. Many seek direction for their lives and ministries without humbly submitting themselves to being a disciple who is willing to learn. Submitting to his will invites us to a place of hearing clearly his direction for our lives. *"Trust in the Lord with all your heart; do not depend on your own understanding. Seek his will in all you do, and he will show you which path to take"* (Proverbs 3:5-6, NLT).

Open your heart to the Word, and allow the embrace of his presence to encourage you.

Open your eyes to the world around you, and allow the brokenness you see to humble you.

Open your hands to be generous, and
prepare for a harvest of blessing to find you.

Open your mind to new and exciting possibilities,
and take a leap of faith into the arms of Jesus
who will never leave you nor forsake you!

Chapter One

Faith

A Personal Faith

*"Faith is not belief without proof, but trust
without reservation."*

—D. Elton Trueblood

Have you personally experienced a redeeming faith
in Christ? Can you say: "I remember when I said yes
to Christ? I remember what happened to me then.
And I remember where I was. It occupies a sacred
place in my life. That was the place where my life was
changed. That's where I chose to follow Christ."

I will always remember Labor Day 1975, when
I went on my first date with my bride-to-be, "Cozy" (Eva
Cosette). I will always remember December 12, 1975,
when we knelt at a sacred altar and became husband
and wife. I will always remember December 26, 1979,
when Steven, our firstborn, came into the world. I will
always remember June 15, 1982, when our youngest
son, Christopher, was born.

I could go on with more important dates (like
the birth of our grandchildren, the day we launched

Christian Life Cathedral, and so on). But for now, just two more pivotal days in my life: I was six years old when I gave my heart to Jesus, and I still remember the time and place when, at fifteen, I said yes to the calling of the Holy Spirit into full-time ministry. Both were very special days for me. I celebrate those times and will always be indebted to the grace of God for His kind leadership in my life.

Remember well those special and sacred moments in your life, and celebrate them often. They make up the framework of the story—your story—that will be told to future generations. I encourage you to write about your life: your purpose, your gifts, and especially the time you gave your heart and life to Jesus. Write about your life so that it can be shared and span generations.

"Remember well those special and sacred moments in your life, and celebrate them often. They make up the framework of the story—your story—that will be told to future generations."

Cozy and I were honored to be the ones to answer their questions and pray with our sons when each of them, at early ages, accepted Christ as their Savior. We marked those days by buying them Bibles and writing the stories of their decisions for Christ in the front pages. Those are moments to celebrate and reflect on often.

A Growing Faith

"Faith is taking the first step even when you don't see the whole staircase."

—Dr. Martin Luther King Jr.

Hebrews 11:1 (NLT) tells us: *"Faith is the confidence that what we hope for will actually happen; it gives us the assurance about things we cannot see."* In becoming fully who God created us to be, faith must be our foundation. This foundation of faith will not only bring success to our lives, but it will also bring us joy in that success. John Wooden, the successful basketball coach, once said, *"There are many things that are essential to arriving at true peace of mind, and one of the most important is faith, which cannot be acquired without prayer."*

Were you created by God to be a businessperson, an educator, to work in government, or to work in construction? Then be the best you can be through study, prayer, and good work discipline.

You were created to work in the ministry of teaching God's Word, as spoken of in Ephesians 4:11: *"Now these are the gifts Christ gave to the church: the apostles, the prophets, the evangelists, and the pastors and teachers."* So be the best you can be through study, prayer, and good work discipline.

On whatever career path your gifts and talents from God lead you, the key to sustain success is faith in God. Building a foundation of faith comes through personal and spiritual discipline. As we study the letters of the apostles to the church we see that as we utilize these disciplines we add increasing faith to our lives.

"Building a foundation of faith comes through personal and spiritual discipline."

This ever-increasing faith happens as we enlarge our capacity for greater things by investing time in knowing Jesus. He promised these "greater things," and we experience them as we grow in the knowledge of him through the personal and spiritual disciplines given to us in the Word of God. The apostle Peter encourages our journey in this manner: *"In view of all this, make every effort to respond to God's promises. Supplement your faith with a generous provision of moral excellence, and moral excellence with knowledge, and knowledge with self-control, and self-control with patient endurance, and patient endurance with godliness, and godliness with brotherly affection, and brotherly affection with love for everyone. The more you grow like this, the more productive and useful you will be in your knowledge of our Lord Jesus Christ"* (2 Peter 1:5-8, NLT).

To grow in faith, it is essential that we know the Christ of our faith. Study of the life, message, and ministry of Christ is more important than any other biblical study you may undertake. This should be our first priority. Study the Gospels. Know the history of those who wrote the Gospels, and become fluent in telling the story of Christ to others. It is truly the "good news."

Knowledge of the Word of God will only increase your ability to succeed. Study with an open heart the beatitudes contained in the Lord's *Sermon on the Mount.* The parables Jesus taught to the crowds who surrounded him will give you an insight into human nature that will help in all you do. Study carefully the miracles that happened as he interacted with hurting people. Seek sincerely to understand his servant's heart so you can serve those around you with joy.

Don't make it difficult! Jesus said in Matthew 11:30 (version), *"My yoke is easy to bear, and the burden I give you is light."* I love this illustration. In the days Jesus walked on earth, it was common to observe oxen being used to plow the fields. The animals were harnessed to a heavy wooden yoke that fit over their shoulders. The yoke was attached to a piece of equipment that plowed the ground as the animals pulled.

The law, taught by the religious leaders of those days, had become so burdensome that the people were worn out and tired from attempting to keep it. Jesus said, "No! Being my friend and a child of God is not burdensome or heavy." He was giving an invitation to discipleship. "Take off the burdensome yoke of religion," Jesus said, "and take my yoke upon you." Thus, we can conclude that his teaching (yoke) was not then, and is not now, burdensome. It is light and life-giving. It is not so deep as to be unattainable, but is instead available and understandable to all who seek to know him intimately.

A Positive Faith

"Faith is to believe what you do not see; the reward of this faith is to see what you believe."

—St. Augustine

Jesus always left the people who sought him in a better state than when he first met them. He gave them hope. Those who were willing to receive were made healthy mentally, physically, emotionally, and spiritually. He gave them a strong sense of confidence, and they knew he loved them. Then, he solidified it all by giving his life for them.

Jesus did not condemn people. He did, however, boldly take a stand against evil in the world and against the self-serving religious systems that control individuals. Learn from Jesus how to treat those with whom you interact with grace, mercy, and compassion. We don't have to take a whip and drive out the money changers, as he did. Learn how to love like Jesus loved so that you may offer love to others as he did. Learn how to love like Jesus loved so that you can heal like Jesus healed.

"Jesus always left the people who sought him in a better state than when he first met them. He gave them hope."

"For this is how God loved the world: He gave his one and only Son, so that everyone who believes in him will not perish but have eternal life. God sent his Son into the world not to judge the world, but to save the world through him. There is no judgment against anyone who believes in him. But anyone who does not believe in him has already been judged for not believing in God's one and only Son" (John 3:16-18, NLT). Inspired by these verses, I have purposed to pray: "Lord help me to live a life of conviction without condemnation, and to have compassion without compromise."

Serving Christ and sharing his love with the world is one of the most positive, energizing actions you will ever have the privilege of taking. Keep it positive, keep it exciting, and celebrate the life that is in Christ with all who find themselves lost and confused by their own transgressions.

We should always promote hope rather than despair, victory rather than defeat, and promise rather than problems. The life of a believer is to be one of joy, not sadness. Living for and with Christ is great, so let us promote it with celebration and excitement! *"Those who look to him for help will be radiant with joy; no shadow of shame will darken their faces"* (Psalm 34:5, NLT).

Joy strengthens us, while shame weakens us. One of my favorite passages in the Word is Hebrews 12:1-3 (NLT): *"Therefore, since we are surrounded by such a huge crowd of witnesses to the life of faith, let us strip off every weight that slows us down, especially the sin that so easily trips us up. And let us run with endurance the race God has set before us. We do this by keeping our eyes on Jesus, the champion who initiates and perfects our faith. Because of the joy awaiting him, he endured the cross, disregarding its shame."*

Various translations say it a little differently. In the phrase "disregarding its shame," the words "despising," "scorning," and "ignoring" are sometimes used. So, because he rejected shame, we now have that same privilege!

This, my friend, is a positive faith that we promote; and the future of the body of Christ, living without the shame of sins forgiven, looks good.

Discussion

1. In practical terms, how can and should faith be put to use in our lives as followers of Christ?

2. What are your thoughts on the "greater things" we can receive as we mature in faith?

3. When you think of God's laws, do you see them as delightful or burdensome? Why?

4. What is the difference between the yoke of religion and the yoke of Christ?

5. How can you help a person who has fallen into "sin" without putting him or her to shame?

Introspection

1. Meditate on some of the moments in your life that are sacred. How have you given them the space in your heart they deserve?

2. In which areas of your life can you improve on self-discipline? How so? What plan can you put into action?

3. Are there areas in your life in which you carry shame? Do you have the skills to resist in these areas of weakness? If not, who do you know who can help you walk through them and into total victory?

Chapter Two

Family

"You don't choose your family. They are God's gift to you, as you are to them."

—Desmond Tutu

Love, forgiveness, encouragement, and celebration are the words that should be used to capture the beautiful image of "family." But in our day the common classification is "dysfunctional." Now, I believe there are many functional families that have some dysfunction within them. In fact, I jokingly tell the folks that attend Christian Life Cathedral (CLC) that all of us are dysfunctional at times, so cut each other some slack! Dysfunction should not paralyze us from moving forward. Some of the most highly significant families in the Word of God had dynamics that screamed dysfunction, yet God still used them mightily.

Rather than focus on the dysfunction that some families deal with, let me draw your attention to some of the positive characteristics of a highly productive family: family members *love* one another, *forgive* one another, *encourage* one another, and *celebrate* one another's successes. These traits can be developed.

The value (or lack of value) we place on our families will greatly affect the way we view others and conduct our lives. It is a reality that needs to be dealt with. As a person committed to spending my life in church ministry, I learned early on that my most important responsibility was to put my family before my ministry. This does not mean I was to put my family before God himself, but that I was to put my family before the work associated with my ministry. It is the same for each of us, no matter the path our gifts and talents take us on. It should always be God first, family second, and vocation after that. We are to honor our families above all else but God. If we honor God with all our hearts, it will be a given that our families will be honored by ourselves and God.

". . . highly productive family: family members *love* one another, *forgive* one another, *encourage* one another, and *celebrate* one another's successes."

My family has graced me over the years because they know and understand my love for them. I am first and foremost a follower of Christ; then a husband, a father, a pastor, a friend, and a counselor. My vocation as a minister of the gospel has led me to regularly wrestle with scriptures regarding family with which, perhaps, people with other vocations do not. But I believe that a life lived for Christ inevitably will lead all of us into this kind of wrestling. Note the following conversation about family that Jesus had with some who desired to follow him. This is found in Luke 9:57-62 (NLT):

As they were walking along, someone said to Jesus, "I will follow you wherever you go." But Jesus replied, "Foxes have dens to live in, and birds have nests, but the Son of Man has no place even to lay his head." He said to another person, "Come, follow me." The man agreed, but he said, "Lord, first let me return home and bury my father." But Jesus told him, "Let the spiritually dead bury their own dead! Your duty is to go and preach about the Kingdom of God." Another said, "Yes, Lord, I will follow you, but first let me say good-bye to my family." But Jesus told him, "Anyone who puts a hand to the plow and then looks back is not fit for the Kingdom of God."

There is a very practical application of this text that has to do with protecting the decision we make to follow Christ and his chosen path for our lives. The plans that family members have for us may not coincide with what God has called us to do. At this point, we are accountable first to what God has called us to do. But we should never use scripture as an excuse to neglect family. I have seen both extremes: family members who refused to honor the vocation of other family members, and those who used their vocation as an opportunity to neglect their family. Both are wrong. Whatever your vocation, include your family and conduct yourself in a way your family can honor.

These words of Jesus sound hard on the surface. Understanding the world around him at the time gives us a better view of the meaning in this scripture. Jesus knew what people were up against when they shared

with their families their desire to follow him. The Jew-
ish family laid out plans for each child's education,
spouse, work, where they would live—basically their
entire lives! Jesus knew strong tradition would dictate
the future for most people.

Perhaps this is true of your circumstance as well. It
is so important for parents to understand the person-
ality, gifts, and talents of their children and to, while
guiding them, allow them the space to become what
they were born to be.

Wisdom in Accountability

Whatever you choose as your vocation, accountability is a basic need for becoming all you can be. It is
our responsibility to find people to whom we can be
accountable in every area of our lives. You probably
will never rise above those with whom you invest your
time, so choose well!

As followers of Christ, it is important that we
make ourselves accountable to a spiritual authority.
It is difficult to choose the path of honor long-term
when we do not have trusted, loving voices of correction, counsel, and rebuke speaking into our lives.
Accountability to those we honor for what their lives
teach us (our mentors) and to those who walk along
beside us (our peers and partners) is a safety net
for our character. It helps us maintain pure hearts,
right motives, and humble attitudes of service and
obedience. Stay true to yourself and listen to the
voices of reason.

Our parents, even as long as they have authority over us, should not be responsible to clean up our

messes (though at times, they have this job). When we reach the age of being accountable, we should *man up* and take responsibility for our own lives.

"It is difficult to choose the path of honor long-term when we do not have trusted, loving voices of correction, counsel, and rebuke speaking into our lives."

I remember when I was just beginning to travel in ministry. I was crossing the desert from Nevada into Northern California, when a tire blew on my vehicle. After putting on the spare, I continued on my way, looking for a service station. I finally saw one and pulled right in, intent on purchasing new tires because I was running on slick all the way around. The man put them on for me. I gave him my credit card, but it was rejected. Embarrassed, I asked the man to patch the one and put my old tires back on.

Later, when my father heard this story, he said, "Steve, all you had to do was telephone me and I would have sent the money." But my father was not responsible for my debts. I was an adult. Lessons learned in the desert places are oftentimes the best lessons.

Spouse and Children

"Love begins at home. Everything depends on how we love each other. Do not be afraid to love until it hurts, for this is how Jesus loved."

—Mother Teresa

I love Cozy Dixon! I thank God daily for her love, her wisdom, and her willingness to be there when I've needed her most. Robert Browning said, "Grow old with me, the best is yet to be. The last of life, for which the first is made."

It is so important that couples build on a foundation of love and respect. If you are married—or are planning for that event—it is very important that you and your partner share like faith and similar expressions of that faith. Your healthiest interaction in matters of faith should be with each other. Work diligently to provide a safe place for each of you to share your deepest thoughts and feelings. Dream together and serve together. Don't make marriage a competition; make it a partnership.

The health of your marriage will either energize your home or deplete your energy and peace. Do all you can to remain loving and giving toward your spouse. There is an order of relationships that God blesses: God first, our spouse and children second, and our vocation third. Don't allow anyone or anything to come between you and God or you and your spouse. The apostle Paul beautifully instructs us in the value of our relationship to our spouse in Ephesians 5:21-30 (NLT):

"The health of your marriage will either energize your home or deplete your energy and peace."

And further, submit to one another out of reverence for Christ. For wives, this means submit to your husbands as to the Lord. For a husband is the head of his wife as Christ is the head of the church. He is the Savior of his body, the church. As the church submits to Christ, so you wives should submit to your husbands in everything. For husbands, this means love your wives, just as Christ loved the church. He gave up his life for her to make her holy and clean, washed by the cleansing of God's word. He did this to present her to himself as a glorious church without a spot or wrinkle or any other blemish. Instead, she will be holy and without fault. In the same way, husbands ought to love their wives as they love their own bodies. For a man who loves his wife actually shows love for himself. No one hates his own body but feeds and cares for it, just as Christ cares for the church. And we are members of his body.

Because my vocation is pastoring, my family has felt at times that they live in a "glass house," that someone is constantly watching them. On the other hand, some families feel neglected because the husband—or even the wife at times—puts vocation before them. We must be careful not to allow this to happen.

Pray daily for your spouse and children. Take quality time away from your job to celebrate your marriage and family. Develop a treasure of memories with each other apart from your work assignment. Life can be wonderful when lived in proper alignment.

Parenting, at best, is one of the most challenging jobs you will ever have in life. But the rewards are so tremendous. Here are just a couple decisions Cozy and I made when we began raising our children that might encourage you:

1. Always keep the conversation positive in the presence of your children. Your hurts and disappointments need to be worked out in private, between your spouse and yourself. Be careful not to influence your children in a negative way toward people in your circle of influence. You never know when that man who is irritating you today will be your kids Little League coach tomorrow!

2. Encourage your children to dream about the things they would like to accomplish in life. Don't let it be assumed that they will follow you in your vocation. Many well-meaning adults attempt to put their dreams—fulfilled or unfulfilled—on their children. Guard them from that undue burden, and at the same time, be sensitive to their gifts and talents. Your children need the same privilege of hearing from God to discover and fulfill their dreams as you did. Wherever God leads them, celebrate it with them!

3. If you want your children to celebrate your vocation, you need to be purposeful in celebrating their vacation away from school. Often, I have heard parents say, "My kids have no appreciation for what we do and how hard we work for them." The best way to counteract that is to celebrate them as often as possible, at home and away from home.

Enjoy your family. Learn to pray together. Have fun together. And whether you have the required rhythm or not, learn to dance so you can honor your child at his or her wedding! I doubt seriously that Jesus stood in the corner at the marriage celebration he attended at Cana, just waiting for his chance to perform a miracle. I think he was there to celebrate the bride and groom with his family and their families.

"Enjoy your family. Learn to pray together. Have fun together. And whether you have the required rhythm or not, learn to dance so you can honor your child at his or her wedding!"

I remember very well the times when we would find my mother and father standing outside the school on special Friday afternoons, waiting to take us (my sister Renee, Greg the preschooler, and me) about sixty miles away from home to a motel for the night. And not just to any motel—it would be one with a nice swimming pool! We would enjoy swimming that night and the next day before heading home so my father could preach on Sunday. Now, this seems a little bizarre, I know, but what we were doing was something that most of the church folks back home would have had difficulty with. The old "mixed bathing" (swimming) issue was a big deal in the church world in the early 1960s. However, my father celebrated his kids, despite the way some of the religious crowd thought. Ridiculous, right? But it was righteously right for us kids! (Thanks, Dad!)

Lighten up! You've got one shot at doing this parenting thing right. You'll make mistakes. Cry and laugh your way through them.

Before we move on from the subject of family, let me address something I believe is very important for generational health in family relationships. Since establishing the church body of Christian Life Cathedral in Fayetteville, Arkansas, my father and I have colabored together there as pastors. The very fact that I am the visionary leader has created a unique environment. My father has always said, "Anything with two heads is a monster." Therefore, role clarification is very important in our situation, as well as in any other successful endeavor.

Several years ago, my father stood before our congregation and made a statement that I will never forget. As a matter of fact, I wrote it in my Bible. He said, "It is my sincere desire and earnest expectation that Steve will accomplish more in life and ministry than I have ever been able to accomplish." As you can imagine, I was deeply humbled that my father would make such a public statement of value concerning my life and ministry. I believe my father sincerely wants his family to succeed in whatever endeavors we have chosen. Just knowing that he wants his children, grandchildren, and great-grandchildren to succeed gives us all a head start on our personal journeys.

Several years ago, when our second son, Christopher, pastored in Texas, I was privileged to speak to his congregation. Fighting back tears, I said to them, "It is my sincere desire and earnest expectation that Christopher will accomplish more in life and ministry than I have ever been able to accomplish." I felt it was the appropriate statement for me to use in affirming my confidence in Christopher's ability to lead.

Our firstborn son, Steven, is a successful business-man in the marketplace. He was born to succeed and be a leader among men in the business world. God continues to bless him in a tremendous way. I let him know often that, "It is my sincere desire and earnest expectation that you will accomplish more in life and ministry than I have ever been able to accomplish." His ministry is business.

God help us, as parents, not to neglect the power of positive prophecy we are privileged to speak over our children! Affirm them often and celebrate them every day of their lives.

Discussion

1. How would you define "dysfunction"?
2. When Jesus says something that feels strange, such as, "Let the dead bury the dead," what can we do to get to his real meaning?
3. In a society that seems out of control in many ways, what are some practical ways to help families stay strong?
4. What are some healthy ways to make our homes a joy for our families?
5. Parenting is difficult at best. What positive actions have you taken that produced good results?

Introspection

1. To whom am I accountable? How honest am I when sharing who I really am?

2. How do I invest my time in quality people and actions?

3. Where does my family rank in my life? Why?

4. What dreams do I have for my family?

Chapter Three

Finances

"If a person gets his attitude toward money straight, it will help straighten out almost every other area in his life."

—Billy Graham

May God always honor your heart and acts of generosity, and may he give you abundant seed to sow! Be careful not to fall into thinking, *I will do [whatever] when God provides the finances.* Start the journey, and God will provide the finances. *"Give to everyone what you owe them: Pay your taxes and government fees to those who collect them, and give respect and honor to those who are in authority. Owe nothing to anyone— except for your obligation to love one another. If you love your neighbor, you will fulfill the requirements of God's law"* (Romans 13:7-8, NLT).

Money can be a great blessing to your life and the lives of your family members, or it can be a tremendous hindrance. It's not a question of having enough money to fulfill the dreams God placed inside you; it's about having the right attitude of wise stewardship with the financial resources you do have.

Money follows a life of giving. Followers of Christ, kingdom believers, shouldn't chase after money for any reason. If we serve people using our God-given talents, he will supply the provision to fulfill the vision. Be in alignment with the Scriptures and make your request known to God, and he will give you ample finances to provide for yourself and your family, with funds left over to give to others. *"If you are faithful in little things, you will be faithful in large ones. But if you are dishonest in little things, you won't be honest with greater responsibilities"* (Luke 16:10, NLT).

When we began Christian Life Cathedral (CLC), we were not able to take a salary because of the various expenses involved in that new venture of faith. I will never forget the week I finally received my modest very first salary check from CLC. I was thrilled!

On my way to the bank to deposit the check, I stopped by the post office to check the mail. Coming out of the post office, I saw a young man who served as a youth pastor at a neighboring church in our city. I had enjoyed some quality fellowship with him over the previous few months, and he had shared with me his young family's financial challenges. I knew he was attempting to use his gifts and talents to work with youth while raising a family, and his salary was inadequate to meet his family's needs. It wasn't that the church where he worked couldn't pay him enough; they just refused to honor any of their pastors with an appropriate salary. When I greeted him and asked how things were going, he held back tears and replied, "Not good."

As his tears began to flow, I asked him to get in my car. He told me, "This morning I opened the kitchen cabinets and saw that we have nothing left for my wife to fix even one meal, and very little is left to feed our child."

As he spoke, I knew that the check (my first salary check) was meant for him and not for me. I pulled that check out of my shirt pocket, signed it over to my young friend, and together we prayed that he would be encouraged to always remember that God was his source.

Within days, that young man received an invitation to join the staff of a church that would appreciate and honor him for his gifts and talents. God again reminded me that he is my source, and that he will provide all I will ever need to do the ministry to which he called me.

I sincerely pray that we will all learn and never forget the value and joy of giving tithes, offerings, and alms. It is equally important to practice discipline with personal savings. These are important commitments that will honor God and enable you to do life and serve your family and circle of influence with confidence.

The Tithe

"God doesn't need us to give him our money. He owns everything. Tithing is God's way to grow Christians."

—Adrian Rogers

"'Bring all the tithes into the storehouse so there will be enough food in my Temple. If you do,' says the Lord of Heaven's Armies, 'I will open the windows of heaven for you. I will pour out a blessing so great you won't have enough room to take it in! Try it! Put me to the test!'" (Malachi 3:10, NLT).

God asks for a tithe of our earnings (literally, a tenth part). The first ten percent belongs to God, and he assures us of a blessing when we release it to him. I believe the "storehouse" is the local church. The leaders of the local church use these tithes to do the ministry to which God has assigned us all, to train and equip the body of Christ to influence and be an example of the kingdom of God to all.

Tithing was instituted long before the law. "*And Melchizedek, the king of Salem and a priest of God Most High, brought Abram some bread and wine. Melchizedek blessed Abram with this blessing: 'Blessed be Abram by God Most High, Creator of heaven and earth. And blessed be God Most High, who has defeated your enemies for you.' Then Abram gave Melchizedek a tenth of all the goods he had recovered*" (Genesis 14:18-20, NLT).

Abram (Abraham) blessed God by giving to King Melchizedek, the priest of Jerusalem, the tithe of all he possessed. This is reemphasized in the law: "*One-tenth of the produce of the land, whether grain from the fields or fruit from the trees, belongs to the Lord and must be set apart to him as holy*" (Leviticus 27:30, NLT).

Jesus also endorsed tithing: "*What sorrow awaits you teachers of religious law and you Pharisees. Hypocrites! For you are careful to tithe even the tiniest income from your herb gardens, but you ignore the more important aspects of the law—justice, mercy, and faith. You should tithe, yes, but do not neglect the more important things*" (Matthew 23:23, NLT).

We should give a tithe of everything that comes our way. We are instructed to practice justice, mercy, faith, *and* tithing. We are to give ten percent of our income.

We are to bring *all* of the tithe into the storehouse. If you are one of the few who are blessed with the privilege of a housing allowance, remember to tithe on *all* of the income and benefits. Don't limit the blessings of God to your finances.

One of the most important principles regarding tithing is to give it first. *"Honor the Lord with your wealth and with the best part of everything you produce. Then he will fill your barns with grain, and your vats will overflow with good wine"* (Proverbs 3:9-10, NLT).

Offerings

"The value of a man resides in what he gives and not in what he is capable of receiving."

—Albert Einstein

The second area of responsibility is that of giving offerings: *"Give to the Lord the glory he deserves! Bring your offering and come into his courts"* (Psalm 96:8, NLT). In the body of Christ, offerings are used to fund buildings, special projects, and various tools necessary for getting the gospel to the ends of the earth. It brings glory to God when we bring an offering as we gather to worship him.

"Jesus called his disciples to him and said, 'I tell you the truth, this poor widow has given more than all the others who are making contributions. For they gave a tiny part of their surplus, but she, poor as she is, has given everything she had to live on' " (Mark 12:43-44, NLT).

This woman was not just paying her tithe; she was giving an offering on top of her tithe. In fact, she gave all of her means. Our sacrifice honors God. Obedience is better than sacrifice, but sacrifice is still considered worship unto the Lord! It's not so much the amount we give that honors God, but rather the amount we have left over. If we are willing to sacrifice to God some of the essential things in our lifestyle, he is certainly honored.

"Give, and you will receive. Your gift will return to you in full—pressed down, shaken together to make room for more, running over, and poured into your lap. The amount you give will determine the amount you get back" (Luke 6:38, NLT).

Giving, in this scripture, involves more than just money. It involves the giving of ourselves. We are to be a true friend to others, going the second mile to do even more than we committed to do. God will reward us generously for such acts of kindness.

Alms

In addition to tithes and offerings, we are also encouraged to give alms.

Jesus placed a great significance on the believer's giving of alms. This gift giving has much to do with the ultimate salvation of others. It is an expression of the kindness of Christ to those who are in need.

"Don't you see how wonderfully kind, tolerant, and patient God is with you? Does this mean nothing to you? Can't you see that his kindness is intended to turn you from your sin?" (Romans 2:4, NLT).

Most of us feel that we've had a near perfect day when we have done something for someone else, and they may not even know we were involved in meeting the need. On December 26, 2004, an earthquake occurred with an epicenter off the west cost of Sumatra,

Indonesia. It was followed by a tsunami; walls of water over 100 feet high lashed the coastline, killing hundreds of thousands of people. A mission organization I belong to went to work immediately to raise funds to help survivors stranded there. Now homeless, many had no way of knowing where their immediate families were, or even if they were alive.

I will never forget standing in Aceh, Indonesia, while delivering our offerings to local churches that were working to help. The devastation was beyond my imagination, and my heart was broken for those precious people. I whispered a prayer, "Father how can we help them?" A truth was solidified in my heart that day that sustains me to this day: "Through kindness. You help them through kindness." Kindness that is rooted in the love of God will not fail to touch and move those who are suffering. Whether a widow in your neighborhood, a single mom attempting to raise children on her own, a divorced dad who is lonely, a gay couple in your community who is being shunned, children in your city who have no shoes or warm clothes to wear to school—kindness is the tool that will reveal Christ to them.

Jesus told us that even a cup of cold water given in his name was seen by God and rewarded. We cannot expect God to bless and prosper us if we turn a deaf ear to the cry of the poor: *"Those who shut their ears to the cries of the poor will be ignored in their own time of need"* (Proverbs 21:13, NLT).

God promises to meet our needs if we will meet the needs of others. It is very important to learn the blessing of giving to the poor and the less fortunate. (God, give us a generous heart, and may we use it well.)

*You know the generous grace of our Lord Jesus
Christ. Though he was rich, yet for your sakes
he became poor, so that by his poverty he could
make you rich. Here is my advice: It would be
good for you to finish what you started a year
ago. Last year you were the first who wanted
to give, and you were the first to begin doing
it. Now you should finish what you started.
Let the eagerness you showed in the beginning be matched now by your giving. Give in
proportion to what you have. Whatever you
give is acceptable if you give it eagerly. And
give according to what you have, not what you
don't have. Of course, I don't mean your giving
should make life easy for others and hard for
yourselves. I only mean that there should be
some equality. Right now you have plenty and
can help those who are in need. Later, they
will have plenty and can share with you when
you need it. In this way, things will be equal.
As the Scriptures say, 'Those who gathered a
lot had nothing left over, and those who gathered only a little had enough.'* " (2 Corinthians
8:9-15, NLT)*

As we learn to give to the poor, God will bless our
lives. However, if we neglect this area of responsibility,
we have done so to one of the most important principles of God's Word. Be a leader among those in your
circle of influence by your own personal expression of
worship and stewardship. Make the commitment to
tithe, to give offerings, and to give alms. If all believers
practiced these three biblical principles of giving, every

need in the church would be met. I believe missionaries and church planters would be completely funded,
and every benevolent outreach would have more than
enough to feed and clothe every hungry and hurting
person. This is a lot to consider, but we can focus on
our own stewardship and on faithfully influencing others in a positive way.

Consider making the following a part of your life,
ministry, attitude, and action:

- Don't let your salary determine your income.
  Rather, let your giving determine your income.
  Your spiritual wealth isn't determined by what
  you have; it's determined by what you give!
- Purpose each year to give more than the previous
  year. Look for creative ways to do this. Make this
  a part of your family fun. Kids will love learning
  to share if you love to share!
- Learn the principles of biblical stewardship, and
  teach others the ways of the generous life in
  Christ.

**"Don't let your salary determine your income.
Rather, let your giving determine your
income."**

---

*"Remember this—a farmer who plants only a few
seeds will get a small crop. But the one who plants
generously will get a generous crop. You must each
decide in your heart how much to give. And don't give
reluctantly or in response to pressure. 'For God loves a*

person who gives cheerfully.' And God will generously provide all you need. Then you will always have everything you need and plenty left over to share with others" (2 Corinthians 9:6-8, NLT).

I approach the subject of generosity with a personal sense of confidence because I have practiced these principles from the time I received my first paycheck. My father taught us the biblical response to giving, and we quickly discovered the joy of living the generous life. My personal testimony is that, over the years, I have proven it to be true that God always honors his Word.

> *"God is a good bookkeeper!"*
>
> —C.L. "Red" Dixon (my father)

Look to God for all of the provision needed for your vision!

Practice biblical principles of giving, and let God be your source. Yes, he will use people, but be careful not to seek man before you seek God. I challenge you to "prove" God.

In our many years of ministry, we have seen missionaries, pastors, evangelists, parachurch, and marketplace ministry leaders raised up and sent out from our congregation. Most of them have said to me in the beginning of their ministry, "Pastor, I just don't like raising funds." Well, I have assured them all that they will most likely be raising funds for the duration of their ministry. It is my responsibility as their pastor to practice biblical giving and instruct others in the same way. If you are a pastor, make friends with teaching and receiving the tithes, offerings, and alms in the local church.

Many years ago one of our elders, Dan Downing, came to me and said, "Pastor, I'm an accountant, and I could be held liable for withholding information that could profit my clients. I encourage you not to withhold teachings on 'giving' that would profit our congregation." If pastors thought we might be held liable, perhaps we would be more diligent in teaching the biblical principles of giving to our people. Some day we will give an account to God for what we teach.

Whatever role in ministry you fulfill, you will most likely be challenged by different ideas and approaches to the subject of giving. Honor the biblical principles of giving for yourself, and then instruct others in the obedience to them.

Obedience to the teachings of the Word of God is our highest offering of worship. There, we are truly saying, "I trust you, Lord."

"Obedience to the teachings of the Word of God is our highest offering of worship."

Discussion

1. What different attitudes have you observed in others concerning money?

2. How can money be a blessing? How can it become a hindrance?

3. How does God use tithing to grow us, spiritually? Twenty percent or less of the body of Christ faithfully tithe. Why?

4. How do family dynamics affect attitudes about tithing and giving? Share an example of sacrificial giving and blessing from it.

5. What are some creative ways to give alms? What are some ways we can teach our children to be givers?

Introspection

1. What is my attitude toward money?

2. What do I feel when given the opportunity to give?

3. How do my words and attitudes display my feelings about the tithe?

4. In my innermost being, am I a giver or a taker? Why?

Chapter Four

Friends

*"Reliable friends who do what they say
are like cool drinks in sweltering heat
– refreshing!"*

(Proverbs 25:13, MSG)

Everybody needs friends! The old television series *Cheers* was about a bunch of friends who met almost every day in a neighborhood bar where "everybody knows your name." When one of them got in trouble, the others showed warmth and sympathy.

We all want to be somewhere where everybody, or at least a few, know our name. Friendship is a priceless gift. There is never a time or season in life when we don't need friends. But know this: true friendships are designed to increase in value as they are lived out. The encouragement of a friend's very presence is immeasurable.

Helen Keller, born blind and deaf, said, *"I would rather walk with a friend in the dark than alone in the light."* Although she was trapped in a silent, dark world, she had a real understanding of friendship.

God has blessed me with many friends, and I am grateful for every one of them. There are those he has brought into my life to be even more to me—supernatural relationships that get stronger as we make this journey through life together. We may not see each other every day at the neighborhood bar, but we have something so much stronger. We share a bond of love for one another that is rooted in our love for Christ. I have learned from these friendships important truths:

- FRIENDS show up for each other
- FRIENDS speak life to each other
- FRIENDS stand up for each other

"There are 'friends' who destroy each other, but a real friend sticks closer than a brother" (Proverbs 18:24, NLT).

Jesus selected twelve men with whom he developed a special friendship. Of the twelve there were three— Peter, James, and John—he invited into an intimate circle of conversation and experience. You will recall that those three were with him in the Garden of Gethsemane the evening of his great trial. That evening he called them away from the other disciples as he prayed: *"Then Jesus went with them to the olive grove called Gethsemane, and he said, 'Sit here while I go over there to pray.' He took Peter and Zebedee's two sons, James and John, and he became anguished and distressed. He told them, 'My soul is crushed with grief to the point of death. Stay here and keep watch with me' "* (Matthew 26:36-38, NLT).

These three were also invited to be with Jesus on the Mount of Transfiguration, where Moses and Elijah appeared with him: *"Six days later Jesus took Peter, James, and John, and led them up a high mountain to be alone. As the men watched, Jesus' appearance was transformed, and his clothes became dazzling white, far whiter than any earthly bleach could ever make them. Then Elijah and Moses appeared and began talking with Jesus"* (Mark 9:2-4, NLT).

Then there was that one, John the beloved, with whom Jesus shared a deep, supernatural friendship. As difficult as it is for us to understand, John himself told the story of how he was the disciple who laid his head on the shoulder of Jesus at the Passover meal the night before his death (John 13:23).

And then there was the moment when Jesus, hanging between life and death, looked at John, and then at his grieving mother, Mary, and said to him, *"Behold your mother."* History tells us that from that day on, John cared for Mary, the mother of Jesus, for as long as she lived.

There was a similar relationship in the Old Testament that models for us supernatural friendships. It is the friendship between David and Jonathan, King Saul's son. Theirs is a beautiful story of a friendship that comforts, counsels, protects, and encourages.

As we read the story of their meeting, we recognize that it was God who drew them together. I believe God desires that we all have supernatural friends in our lives—those he brings to us so that we can assist each other in being the best we can be.

David, a young man, moves suddenly from a home of seven brothers and the daily task of taking care of sheep, to living in the palace with the king and his family. David is thrown into a place where the living conditions may have been easier, but the ideology of Saul's family would have been completely different from the one in which David had grown up. He needed a friend, and God gave him Jonathan. Their friendship was stronger than that of their relationship with their families. God gives us friendships that will help us to accomplish our God-given purpose and destiny.

If you don't have such rich friendships, pray that God will bring them to you and that you will be sensitive to his leading. Don't miss the gift he desires to give you.

For the full story of David and Jonathan, read 1 Samuel: 18-20. The verses below describe the beginning of their friendship: *"After David had finished talking with Saul, he met Jonathan, the king's son. There was an immediate bond between them, for Jonathan loved David. From that day on Saul kept David with him and wouldn't let him return home. And Jonathan made a solemn pact with David, because he loved him as he loved himself. Jonathan sealed the pact by taking off his robe and giving it to David, together with his tunic, sword, bow, and belt"* (1 Samuel 18:1-4, NLT).

Here are three questions to ponder:

- Do I have quality friends in my life?
- Do I value those friends the way I would like to be valued?
- Do I pray for and bless my friends?

We need to always celebrate the gift of friendship. Guard the gift of friendship. Teach others the joy of friendship. Be a friend!

I have been asked about close friendships with nonbelievers. Many nonbelievers are absolutely great people, and there is nothing wrong with building strong friendships with them. Any quality relationship should be formed because we genuinely care for the other person.

When you have nonbelieving friends, just be sure to ask yourself if the friendship is a life-giving relationship, or if it is distracting you from your relationship with Christ, your family, and/or your purpose? Don't be fearful of developing close, meaningful friendships, but do guard your heart and pray for discernment.

True friendships are a priceless gift to us. God doesn't want you to journey alone. I heard it said many years ago that everyone needs four specific people in their lives: a model, a mentor, a partner, and a friend.

Make it a matter of prayer that God will bring quality friendships into your life. Also pray that you would become the kind of friend that you desire someone else to be to you.

"I cannot even imagine where I would be today were it not for that handful of friends who have given me a heart full of joy. Let's face it; friends make life a lot more fun!"

—Charles Swindoll

"Friends love through all kinds of weather, and families stick together in all kinds of trouble."

(Proverbs 17:17, MSG)

*"Don't leave your friends or your parents'
friends and run home to your family when
things get rough; Better a nearby friend than
a distant family."*

(Proverbs 27:10, MSG)

*"You use steel to sharpen steel, and one
friend sharpens another."*

(Proverbs 27:17, MSG)

*"This is the very best way to love. Put your
life on the line for your friends."*

(John 15:13, MSG)

"Keep on loving your friends..."

(Psalm 36:10, MSG)

Discussion

1. Share an example from your life when you observed or experienced a greatly valued friendship.

2. Read Proverbs 18:24 aloud. How can friends destroy one another?

3. What are some attributes of supernatural friendships?

4. In the story of Jonathan and David, what kind of man was Jonathan that he was willing to step back and allow God to choose David to take his place as the future king?

5. What is the difference between a model and a mentor?

Introspection

1. Am I a great friend to anyone? How do I show it?
2. Three questions to ponder:
   - Do I have quality friends in my life?
   - Do I value those friends the way I would like to be valued?
   - Do I pray for and bless my friends?
3. Am I mentoring anyone? Do I have a mentor?

Chapter Five

Fruit

"Did I offer peace today? Did I bring a smile to someone's face? Did I say words of healing? Did I let go of my anger and resentment? Did I forgive? Did I love? These are the real questions. I must trust that the little bit of love that I sow now will bear many fruits, here in this world and the life to come."

—Henri Nouwen

"I am the true grapevine, and my Father is the gardener. He cuts off every branch of mine that doesn't produce fruit, and he prunes the branches that do bear fruit so they will produce even more. You have already been pruned and purified by the message I have given you. Remain in me, and I will remain in you. For a branch cannot produce fruit if it is severed from the vine, and you cannot be fruitful unless you remain in me.

Yes, I am the vine; you are the branches. Those who remain in me, and I in them, will produce much fruit. For apart from me you can do

nothing. Anyone who does not remain in me is thrown away like a useless branch and withers. Such branches are gathered into a pile to be burned. But if you remain in me and my words remain in you, you may ask for anything you want, and it will be granted! When you produce much fruit, you are my true disciples. This brings great glory to my Father."
(John 15:1-8, NLT)

Have you ever seen a fruit factory? You might have seen a furniture factory, but you have not seen a fruit factory. You can only find fruit on the tree that bears it. Fruit grows; it is not built. There is no fruit without life. In Galatians 5:25 (NLT), Scripture says, *"Since we are living by the Spirit, let us follow the Spirit's leading in every part of our lives."* He is our lifeline. We cannot manufacture fruit. The fruit of the Spirit is planted in our lives as a gift from God at our spiritual birth, and grow as we remain in him and draw on all the spiritual nourishment he provides.

Dietrich Bonhoeffer said, *"Fruit is always the miraculous, the created; it is never the result of willing, but always a growth. The fruit of the Spirit is a gift of God, and only He can produce it. They who bear it know as little about it as the tree knows of its fruit. They know only the power of Him on whom their life depends."* God desires that we 'bear much fruit.'

Paul gave us a list of the fruit of the Spirit in Galatians. What are they? *"But the Holy Spirit produces this kind of fruit in our lives: love, joy, peace, patience, kindness, goodness, faithfulness, gentleness, and self-control. There is no law against these things! Those who belong to Christ Jesus have nailed the passions and desires of their sinful nature to his cross and crucified them there. Since we are living by the Spirit, let us follow the Spirit's leading in every part of our lives"* (Galatians 5:22-25, NLT).

We will not grow to bear the fruit of the Spirit until we are willing to walk in the Spirit to the point of abiding in the vine, Christ Jesus. Only then will we bear the fruit that the Holy Spirit desires to produce in our lives. Jesus told us that when we abide in him, we will be fruitful. Spiritual formation is that process of learning how to walk in friendship with the Holy Spirit, trusting not in our own efforts to produce spiritual fruit, but resting in his unique ability to produce the fruit he desires for us to bear.

It is very important to remember that the fruit of the spirit is intended to come and remain, whereas the gifts of the spirit come to us as God so chooses to use them in our lives as we serve others. While both are very important, the fruit of the Spirit must be living in us before we can effectively move in the gifts of the Spirit.

Kindness, for instance, is a fruit of the Spirit, and any gift God would give us for advancing his kingdom must be administered in kindness, or else it may be abusive. We are to use the gifts of the Spirit in the same attitude with which we would the fruit of the Spirit. The progression then is this: roots, fruits, and then gifts. First, we are to be rooted and grounded in the love of Christ, and then we bear fruit that will last. Then, I believe God graces us with the gifts of the Spirit at his discretion, according to his wisdom.

The true Christian life has nine visible attributes— the fruit of the Spirit. This is very important for us to understand. We are to follow the Spirit's leading in every part of our lives. This fruit will provide an attitude that is pleasing to the Lord and inviting to others. Who can resist the love of Christ, the first of the fruit of the Spirit?

Discussion

1. Read aloud the pruning process described in John 15. What do you think of this?
2. Tell of a time when the pruning of God changed the path you were on and took you in a more healthy direction.
3. How does the fruit of the Spirit grow in our lives? Are there ways we can nurture the fruit to make it grow?
4. When Paul said there was "no law" against the fruit of the Spirit, what did he mean?
5. Why is it important for the fruit of the spirit to abide in us as we minister in the gifts of the Spirit?

Introspection

1. When I read Henry Nouwen quote, how does my soul answer?
2. Am I willing to pray, "God prune me, that I may grow in you"? Why?

Chapter Six

Love, Joy, and Peace

"What makes us human is not our mind but our heart, not our ability to think but our ability to love."

—Henri Nouwen

Love

The world will know that we are followers of Christ by the fruit of the Spirit manifest in our lives. And it seems that the first fruit mentioned is the primary fruit from which the others gain expression: love (*agape*). In fact, 1 John 4:8 tells us emphatically, *"God is love."*

According to the apostle Paul's description of *agape* love in 1 Corinthians 13:4-13 (NLT):

> *Love is patient and kind. Love is not jealous or boastful or proud or rude. It does not demand its own way. It is not irritable, and it keeps no record of being wronged. It does not rejoice about injustice but rejoices whenever the truth wins out.*

Love never gives up, never loses faith, is always hopeful, and endures through every circumstance.

Prophecy and speaking in unknown languages and special knowledge will become useless. But love will last forever!

Now our knowledge is partial and incomplete, and even the gift of prophecy reveals only part of the whole picture!

But when full understanding comes, these partial things will become useless.

When I was a child, I spoke and thought and reasoned as a child. But when I grew up, I put away childish things.

Now we see things imperfectly as in a cloudy mirror, but then we will see everything with perfect clarity. All that I know now is partial and incomplete, but then I will know everything completely, just as God now knows me completely.

Three things will last forever—faith, hope, and love—and the greatest of these is love.

And John, the "disciple whom Jesus loved, wrote this: 2 John 1:5-6 (NLT) *I am writing to remind you, dear friends, that we should love one another. This is not a new commandment, but one we have had from the beginning. Love means doing what God has commanded us, and he has commanded us to love one another, just as you heard from the beginning.*

With the foundation of love in mind, let's look at the fruit of joy and peace.

Joy

The Greek word for "joy" is *chara*, which is a derivative of *charis*. *Charis* is the Greek word that means "grace." God graces us with his joy, and true joy is a fruit that others see in our everyday living. Joy is not human-based happiness that comes and goes based on temporary surroundings; it is divine in its origin. It is a Spirit-given expression that flourishes best in hard times. Think about this: the persecution they suffered for the sake of Christ brought them joy. The opening letter to the church in 1 Thessalonians 1:6-7 (NLT) says; *"So you received the message with joy from the Holy Spirit in spite of the severe suffering it brought you. In this way, you imitated both us and the Lord. As a result, you have become an example to all the believers in Greece—throughout both Macedonia and Achaia."*

Nehemiah spoke to the people: *" 'Go and celebrate with a feast of rich foods and sweet drinks, and share gifts of food with people who have nothing prepared. This is a sacred day before our Lord. Don't be dejected and sad, for the joy of the Lord is your strength!' And the Levites, too, quieted the people, telling them, 'Hush! Don't weep! For this is a sacred day.' So the people went away to eat and drink at a festive meal, to share gifts of food, and to celebrate with great joy because they had heard God's words and understood them"* Nehemiah 8:10-12, (NLT).

Peace

The fruit of peace is the result of resting in your relationship with God. After losing all his money in the Great Chicago Fire of 1871, Horatio Spafford put his wife and four daughters on a ship crossing the Atlantic. He planned to finish up his business dealings and follow them a few days later. Tragically, the ship carrying his wife and daughters sank. He received a telegram from his wife, who had survived, that said, "Saved alone . . ." Going to meet his wife, he passed near the area where the ship had sunk. Mr. Spafford stood on the deck of the ship and penned the famous hymn, "It is Well with My Soul":

> *When peace, like a river, attendeth my way,*
> *When sorrows like sea billows roll;*
> *Whatever my lot, Thou hast taught me to say,*
> *It is well, it is well with my soul.*

Peace. It is a quietness of spirit—a state of rest—that comes in any storm when you rest in God. Peace is the opposite of chaos and brokenness. The word "peace" comes from the Greek word, *eirene*, which is equivalent to the Hebrew word, *shalom*. *Shalom* expresses the idea of wholeness, completeness, or tranquility in the soul unaffected by outward circumstances or pressures.

"Peace. It is a quietness of spirit—a state of rest—that comes in any storm when you rest in God."

When a person is embraced by peace, he or she has a calm inner stability that results in the ability to conduct himself or herself peacefully—even in the midst of circumstances that would normally be nerve-racking, traumatic, or very upsetting. Jesus, the Prince of Peace, brings peace to the hearts of those who desire it. He said, *"I am leaving you with a gift—peace of mind and heart. And the peace I give is a gift the world cannot give. So don't be troubled or afraid"* (John 14:27, NLT). Peace is not the absence of conflict, but the presence of God no matter what the conflict.

Discussion

1. Compare various kinds of love. How is *agape* different?
2. Read 1 Corinthians 4-7 aloud. How could we better exemplify these characteristics to the world?
3. What is the difference between joy and happiness?
4. Give examples of people who exhibited joy while under persecution.
5. How would you describe the peace of God as the presence of God?

Introspection

1. When I look closely at the fruit of love in 1 Corinthians 13, do I see weaknesses in my life that need to be strengthened?
2. Is my life lived joyfully?
3. Do I live peacefully in a chaotic world?

Chapter Seven

Patience, Kindness, and Goodness

"Never cut a tree down in the wintertime. Never make a negative decision in the low time. Never make your most important decisions when you are in your worst moods. Wait. Be patient. The storm will pass. The spring will come."

—Robert H. Schuller

Patience

Patience. Various translations of the Bible use words such as "long-suffering" or "endurance," but "patience" covers it very well. Looking more deeply, we see that a further meaning of the Greek word *makrothumia* is, "the ability to endure persecution and ill treatment." It describes a person who has the power to exercise revenge, but instead exercises restraint. Saint Frances de Sales wrote, *"Have patience with all things, but first of all with yourself."*

Only a man who had maturity in the fruit of patience could have endured the tests that carried the apostle to that island of Patmos: *"I, John, am your brother and your partner in suffering and in God's Kingdom and in the patient endurance to which Jesus calls us. I was exiled to the island of Patmos for preaching the word of God and for my testimony about Jesus",* (Revelation 1:9, NLT).

Patience will serve you well as you learn to wait on God's timing. For instance, waiting for peace to prepare the way for you, or waiting for a harvest to come in the right season, are imperative as you grow to maturity in the Lord. You will frustrate yourself and others if you do not learn to exercise great patience. Thank God that he has shown great patience with us!

Peter, who was probably the most impulsive of all of Christ's twelve apostles, said this after he had matured in his faith: *"The Lord isn't really being slow about his promise, as some people think. No, he is being patient for your sake. He does not want anyone to be destroyed, but wants everyone to repent"* (2 Peter 3:9, NLT).

And the writer of Hebrews cautioned us this way: *"So do not throw away this confident trust in the Lord. Remember the great reward it brings you! Patient endurance is what you need now, so that you will continue to do God's will. Then you will receive all that he has promised"* (Hebrews 10:35-36, NLT).

Kindness

"Kindness is the language which the deaf can hear and the blind can see."

—Mark Twain

Kindness, from the Greek word *chrestotes,* means, "acting for the good of people regardless of what they do." Kindness is goodness in action, gentleness in dealing with others, and benevolence. The word describes the ability to act for the welfare of those taxing your patience. Those who demonstrate the qualities of kindness are considered to be compassionate, considerate, sympathetic, humane, or gentle.

"So we keep on praying for you, asking our God to enable you to live a life worthy of his call. May he give you the power to accomplish all the good things your faith prompts you to do. Then the name of our Lord Jesus will be honored because of the way you live, and you will be honored along with him. This is all made possible because of the grace of our God and our Lord, Jesus Christ" (2 Thessalonians 1:11-12, NLT).

Kindness is doing something and not expecting anything in return. It is being respectful of and helping others without waiting for someone to give you something in return. Nothing is more gratifying than helping someone in distress and knowing you will never receive any reward from man. Know that God keeps good records.

"Get rid of all bitterness, rage, anger, harsh words, and slander, as well as all types of evil behavior. Instead, be kind to each other, tenderhearted, forgiving one another, just as God through Christ has forgiven you" (Ephesians 4:31-32, NLT).

I have come to appreciate the power of kindness in action. The body of Christ is the most benevolent group of individuals on the planet. They are always the first on the scene when disasters happen anywhere in the world. It is good to remember that any act of kindness we extend will eventually reap a harvest of righteousness.

"Don't you see how wonderfully kind, tolerant, and patient God is with you? Does this mean nothing to you? Can't you see that his kindness is intended to turn you from your sin?" (Romans 2:4, NLT).

Henri Nouwen, who spent his latter years working with those who were the most unlovely in the eyes of the world said, "For Jesus, there are no countries to be conquered, no ideologies to be imposed, no people to be dominated. There are only children, women, and men to be loved."

I believe kindness is the pathway to every person's heart.

"I believe kindness is the pathway to every person's heart."

Goodness

*"Surely your goodness and unfailing love
will pursue me all the days of my life, and
I will live in the house of the LORD forever."
(Psalms 23:6 (NLT)*

This fruit of goodness, from the Greek word *agathosune*, is critical in our spiritual maturity. The world is so tired of mean Christians who, with a Pharisaical spirit, declare loudly in churches and marketplaces, "Do what I say . . . or else."

Many seek hard after the glory of God and miss the glorious privilege of knowing the fullness of his goodness. Moses asked God to show him his glory; he wanted to look upon the face of God. In his humanness, Moses was asking for something God could not or would not allow. But he allowed Moses to see real beauty, the fullness of his goodness. I love this portion of Scripture:

> *Moses responded, "Then show me your glorious presence." The Lord replied, "I will make all my goodness pass before you, and I will call out my name, Yahweh, before you. For I will show mercy to anyone I choose, and I will show compassion to anyone I choose. But you may not look directly at my face, for no one may see me and live." The Lord continued, "Look, stand near me on this rock. As my glorious presence passes by, I will hide you in the crevice of the rock and cover you with my hand until I have passed by. Then I will remove my hand and let you see me from behind. But my face will not be seen." (Exodus 33:18-23, NLT)*

This is truly amazing! Moses wanted to see God's glorious presence, and God told him, "My glorious presence resides in my goodness." Do we want to be in the center of God's glorious presence? We should follow the example of Jesus described in Acts 10:38: *"Jesus went around doing good."*

Many times we think our occasional good deeds do little for the kingdom of God. Desmond Tutu said, "Do your little bit of good where you are; it's those little bits of good put together that overwhelm the world."

I believe the fullness of God's goodness is tangible evidence of his glory with us. The body of Christ is to be the living, active witness of God's glory. How? Through our willingness to minister his goodness to all.

Discussion

1. Read the Robert Schuller quote above. Why is this wisdom important?

2. Why did St. Francis say, "First of all be patient with yourself"?

3. When have your timing and God's timing not coincided? How did you deal with the waiting period?

4. Share a kind action another person made toward you and the difference it made in your life.

5. Moses asked God to show him his glory, and God showed him his goodness. How does the church live up to this revelation?

Introspection

1. Can I truly define myself as a patient person? Why? Where do I need improvement?

2. How seriously have I lived out Ephesians 4:31-32?

3. Jesus went about "doing good." How am I a reflection of Jesus to my world?

Chapter Eight

Faithfulness, Gentleness, and Self-Control

Faithfulness

"Be faithful in small things because it is in them that your strength lies."

—Mother Teresa

Faithfulness, the Greek word *pistis*, means, "committing oneself to something or someone." For instance, committing to being faithful to one's spouse, to the Lord, or even to a cause or one's life work. The very word "faithful" brings us a picture of loyalty and fidelity.

Being faithful requires personal resolve not to wander away from commitments or promises. It's not always easy to be faithful. Christian faith requires trust in God.

"I pray that from his glorious, unlimited resources he will empower you with inner strength through his Spirit. Then Christ will make his home in your hearts as you trust in him. Your roots will grow down into God's love and keep you strong" (Ephesians 3:16-17, NLT).The fruit of faith grows in our lives as we keep looking to

Jesus, and away from all that could distract us from a life of faithfulness. The writer of the **letter to the Hebrews** describes it this way: *"And let us run with perseverance the race marked out for us, fixing our eyes on Jesus, the pioneer and perfecter of faith. For the joy set before him he endured the cross, scorning its shame, and sat down at the right hand of the throne of God. Consider him who endured such opposition from sinners, so that you will not grow weary and lose heart"* (Hebrews 12:1-3, NIV).

Jesus lived faithful to his mission on earth all the way to and through life and death on the cross. He was so focused on his purpose that he did not allow even the shame of nakedness on the cross to distract him. He perfected the fruit of faithfulness in his life on earth so that we can live out our life journey with faithfulness, connected to the vine.

St. Augustine said, "By faithfulness we are collected and wound up into unity within ourselves, whereas we had been scattered abroad in multiplicity." In other words, as we walk in the discipline of the fruit of faithfulness, all the confusion and stress of life will slowly dissipate and peace will become our faithful friend.

Gentleness

"Men sometimes speak as if humility and meekness would rob us of what is noble and bold and manlike. O that all would believe that this is the nobility of the kingdom of heaven, that this is the royal spirit that the King of heaven displayed, that this is Godlike, to humble oneself, to become the servant of all!"

—Andrew Murray

In the Greek, *prautes* is commonly known as "meekness," which is a *divinely balanced* virtue that can only operate through faith. The *New Spirit-Filled Life Bible* defines gentleness as, "A disposition that is even-tempered, tranquil, balanced in spirit, unpretentious, and that has the passions under control. The word is best-translated meekness, not as an indication of weakness, but of power and strength under control. The person who possesses this quality pardons injuries, corrects faults, and rules his own spirit well."

Paul told us, *"Brothers and sisters, if someone is caught in a sin, you who live by the Spirit should restore that person gently. But watch yourselves, or you also may be tempted. Carry each other's burdens, and in this way you will fulfill the law of Christ"* (Galatians 6:1-2, NIV).

Nothing attracts a troubled soul like a person who displays a gentle spirit. We live in a world of confusion, where many times, even we of the household of faith demonstrate anger and harshness. It should not be so.

Nothing attracts a troubled soul like a person who displays a gentle spirit.

If we find ourselves revealing attributes of the flesh, as opposed to the fruit of gentleness, we need to take a timeout. I quote again St. Francis de Sales, who said, *"Nothing is so strong as gentleness, nothing so gentle as real strength."* As ambassadors of the gentlest man who ever walked on earth, we must take time to develop in the sweet fruit of gentleness.

Self-Control

"I have learned that I really do have disci-
pline, self-control, and patience. But they
were given to me as a seed, and it's up to me
to choose to develop them."

—Joyce Meyer

The Greek word used in Galatians 5:23 is *egkra-teia*, which means, "having command, mastery over, and possession of one's own behavior." The fruit of the Spirit of self-discipline is given to us in seed form, and then we grow by partnering with the Holy Spirit in making right choices while working to accomplish our Creator's plan for our lives. It is not easy, but it is important! Solomon told us in Proverbs 25:28 (NLT), *"A person without self-control is like a city with broken-down walls."* Have you seen buildings that have been neglected and fallen into disrepair? That's what a life driven by emotions and without self-control is like: broken, allowing the passions of the moment to direct it wherever the wind blows.

Understand that God created us to be passionate human beings. Self-control is the ability to control the expression of our passions. I am reminded of the Dr. Seuss verse Cozy read to the boys when they were small: *"You have brains in your head . . . you have feet in your shoes . . . you can steer yourself any direction you choose."* The discipline is in the choice.

We all know how little self-discipline Peter had when he first began following Jesus. Often, while reading the narratives in the Gospels, we wonder what Jesus saw in him. He was impetuous to a fault. But in his wisdom, God saw the seeds in Peter that would some-day be used to help establish his church on earth. I want to close this chapter by looking at Peter's words and seeing him as a man who, with the help of the Holy Spirit, had matured in the fruit of the Spirit.

> *By his divine power, God has given us every-thing we need for living a godly life. We have received all of this by coming to know him, the one who called us to himself by means of his marvelous glory and excellence. And because of his glory and excellence, he has given us great and precious promises. These are the promises that enable you to share his divine nature and escape the world's corrup-tion caused by human desires. In view of all this, make every effort to respond to God's promises. Supplement your faith with a gener-ous provision of moral excellence, and moral excellence with knowledge, and knowledge with self-control, and self-control with patient endurance, and patient endurance with godli-ness, and godliness with brotherly affection, and brotherly affection with love for everyone. The more you grow like this, the more produc-tive and useful you will be in your knowledge of our Lord Jesus Christ. (2 Peter 1:3-8, NLT)*

The sin of neglect is too obvious in the body of Christ. God has given all a measure of faith—faith to believe, faith to grow, faith to become the mature, grounded disciple of Christ that we all desire to become. Let us choose well. Let us choose self-discipline.

Discussion

1. How is our commitment to the teachings of Christ reflected in our lives?
2. What did faithfulness look like in the life of Jesus?
3. Why have so many bought into the idea that meekness is weakness?
4. What does a gentle or meek life look like?
5. What does a lack of self-control look like in a person's life? How can self-control be developed?

Introspection

1. Do I think of myself as a faithful person?
2. Do I keep my eyes on Jesus, or on the problems I constantly deal with?
3. Am I willing to carry other people's burdens?
4. Do I live a disciplined life? Why?

Chapter Nine

Favor

"God is working behind the scenes, arranging things in your favor. He is making a way where you don't see a way."

—Joel Osteen

The story of God's favor toward Samuel, the last prophet of the Lord to Israel, can only be fully realized if we see the faithfulness of his mother Hannah. One day, Hannah visited the Temple of God, where she wept with deep anguish, her desire for a son was so strong. God heard and granted her favor. She gave birth to a son and named him Samuel, which means, "Heard from God." In her gratitude, she gave him back to God.

The day came when Hannah fulfilled the promise she had made to God. She took Samuel to the Temple and left him there to serve and minister with Eli the high priest. One night, Samuel was sleeping in the tabernacle, near the ark of God, when he heard his name being called. He ran to Eli to see what he needed. Eli said, "Go back to sleep, I did not call." After this happened the third time, Eli understood God was calling the boy and he told him what to do. The next time the voice called, Samuel said, "Speak Lord, your servant is listening." God spoke. Samuel listened. But that was just the beginning. First Samuel 2:26 (NLT) tells us, *"The boy Samuel grew taller and grew in favor with the Lord and with the people."* Samuel served as a bridge between the prophets and the kings of the Old Testament. In fact, God used this very man to anoint the young shepherd boy, David.

As a very young man living in Los Angeles County, California, I knew my vocational calling from the Lord was full-time ministry, serving God's people first as an evangelist and then as pastor. At that time, I didn't really have the wisdom to know how and where to begin. To be really honest, I felt anxious about the whole thing. One day, my father said, "Let me call a couple guys." He called his friend, Gene Jackson, who pastored in Hendersonville, Tennessee. Gene agreed to have me in for a weeklong revival, and then I saw in detail how God's favor works.

When the meeting was finished, I had nothing else on the calendar for the next week, but Gene graciously asked me to accompany him to a statewide Assemblies of God Camp Meeting, where I was asked to minister in song every night—*every* night! At the end of the week, I had new meetings scheduled, and the rest is history. God's favor came through one phone call made by my father, who was a faithful man of God.

I have often told people that the wisest move they could ever make was to "follow favor." The principle of favor is this: one door could very well open two doors. One job well done may open multiple doors of opportunity—even opportunities you never expected. I call that favor, and I attempt to follow it.

Everyone loves when favor comes his or her way! It is that moment when something you have dreamed of but thought might never happen just seems to fall in your lap. Exactly what am I talking about? Favor: that gracious, friendly action, freely granted, that helps move you toward your dream.

"The principle of favor is this: one door could very well open two doors. One job well done may open multiple doors of opportunity—even opportunities you never expected."

The writer of Proverbs had a lot to say about favor. *"For whoever finds me (wisdom) finds life and receives favor from the Lord"* (Proverbs 8:35, NLT, parentheses added). In Proverbs 3:3-4 (NLT) we read: *"Never let loyalty and kindness leave you! Tie them around our neck as a reminder. Write them deep within your heart. Then you will find favor with both God and people, and you will earn a good reputation."*

In light of the above scriptures, here are a couple questions for consideration: Where does favor come from? How is it obtained?

I'll break it down. First, favor comes from the Lord when we listen to and learn from the voice of wisdom. Favor finds us as we purpose to write Christlike virtues such as loyalty and kindness on the tablet of our heart, deep within our innermost being. And its benefits are incredible. We discover *"favor with both God and people,"* and we *"earn a good reputation."*

During our life journey, there are many occasions in which we are called upon to make critical, and sometimes life-changing, decisions. During these times, it is important we seek peace of mind and spiritual peace through prayer. This often comes through spending time in the Word of God. Don't proceed until you have this supernatural peace. The peace of God will enable you to see the hand of the Lord leading and guiding you. You will realize it is the favor of God that you didn't exactly ask for, but He graciously gave to you simply because he is a good God. God wants his plan and purpose to be done in the earth much more than we could ever want it.

Please note that I am not saying favor will keep you from trials, or even pain. But favor gives you peace and enables you to know that God is with you through difficult times, and that he will bring you through in his victory. There is an incredible energy that comes with living and moving in the favor of the Lord. Favor will produce in us the confidence that is needed to live victoriously under any circumstances.

This scripture reminds me of how God helped Cozy and I purchase our first home: *"The LORD directs the steps of the godly. He delights in every detail of their lives"* (Psalm 37:23, NLT).

I had been traveling for years doing evangelistic meetings when I met Cozy. We were married in 1975 and continued traveling. I often told people we were homeless, but in fact, we were one step up: we lived in hotel or motel rooms.

After three years on the road together, we knew we needed a place we could go to for downtime: we needed some sense of home. We were attracted to northwest Arkansas, where Cozy was raised and my father had pastored when I was a boy. Evangelists' salaries were obviously not stable, so our credit line was just about nonexistent. At one meeting we held in Fayetteville, a couple heard we were looking to buy a house. They were getting ready to move and wanted to sell.

They asked us to look at their home. It was perfect for us! They asked for $18,500. (Remember those 1970s prices?) We went to the bank. No way—they would only approve us for $15,000. We told the people we could not qualify. However, they really wanted us to have the house, so they said, "Here's what we can do: we will sell for $18,000, carry the note for the $3,000, and give you all our furniture."

We got everything! We got our first home—fully furnished—paid off the side note in a year, and finally had a place to call home and retreat to when needed. It was all due to favor from God. I tell people our first home was a miracle that found us. Let your miracle find you. We prayed, and the house found us.

"For the Lord delights in his people; he crowns the humble with victory" (Psalm 149:4, NLT). *"When people's lives please the Lord, even their enemies are at peace with them"* (Proverbs 16:7, NLT). That's his favor! Follow peace and favor will find you. Then walk with confidence through the doors that God opens for you.

- **Trust favor.** Recognize those God has graced to speak into your life.

- **Respect Favor.** Rejoice, knowing that God will supernaturally open doors that no one can close.

- **Learn from favor**. Generosity is a by-product of favor that creates a new standard by which to live.

Favor is the amazing, undeserved benefit of being God's child. He wants to bless, help, and promote us. He wants to treat us as special.

"What shall we say about such wonderful things as these? If God is for us, who can ever be against us? Since he did not spare even his own Son but gave him up for us all, won't he also give us everything else?" (Romans 8:31-32, NLT).

Over and over in God's Word we see his favor being granted to those who have chosen to follow him. Often, favor as the world sees it may look almost late, but understand that God's timing and ours is different.

At the lowest intersection of her life, after her husband had died, Ruth followed God and her mother-in-law to a land she did not know. God's favor brought her into the field Boaz owned. Boaz had heard of this girl who left all she had to help her mother-in-law. He admired her devotion to Naomi, and after a time, came to love her and took her for his wife. While living on earth, Ruth never realized she would one day be admired as the great-grandmother of King David. The story of Ruth is a story of God's love and favor.

David, the shepherd boy who trusted God so completely he could kill giants, found favor with God and man. The "goodness and mercy" he wrote of while watching his father's sheep certainly did follow him all of his days:

> *"The Lord is my shepherd; I have all that I need. He lets me rest in green meadows; he leads me beside peaceful streams. He renews my strength. He guides me along right paths, bringing honor to his name. Even when I walk*

through the darkest valley, I will not be afraid,
for you are close beside me. Your rod and your
staff protect and comfort me. You prepare a
feast for me in the presence of my enemies.
You honor me by anointing my head with oil.
My cup overflows with blessings. Surely your
goodness and unfailing love (kindness, favor,
mercy) will pursue me all the days of my life,
and I will live in the house of the Lord forever."
(Psalm 23, NLT, parentheses added)

Anyone studying the life of David understands that his life had many ups and downs, but God continually guided him to places of favor.

The New Testament begins with a young girl, Mary, who found favor with God becoming the mother of the Christ child. The apostles, men from every walk of life (not exactly the cream of the crop of society), found favor, and the Church of Jesus was established.

Jesus himself possessed many traits that should be part of every Christian's character. From his youth, he was interested in spiritual things. In the second chapter of Luke, the story is told of a time when Jesus, his mother Mary, and earthly father Joseph traveled to Jerusalem to celebrate Passover. When they left to go home to Nazareth, Mary and Joseph assumed Jesus was with them, as they were traveling with a large group. But he was not.

They hurried back to Jerusalem and found him in the Temple, talking about scripture with the spiritual leaders. When his mother asked him why he had done such a thing, and that she and his father had searched for him frantically, he answered, *"Didn't you know that I must be in my Father's house?"* But he returned home with them, Luke tells us. The Bible says this: *"Then he returned to Nazareth with them and was obedient to them. And his mother stored all these things in her heart. Jesus grew in wisdom and in stature and in favor with God and all the people"* (Luke 2:51-52, NLT).

The four areas we Jesus grew in were wisdom, stature, favor with God, and favor with all people. And we are to do the same. God has already provided all the favor we will ever need. However, just as Jesus had to grow in favor, so do we. As we mature in the principles of faithfulness and obedience, we can expect to grow in favor with both God and men, just as Jesus did.

> *"And may the Lord our God show us his*
> *approval and make our efforts successful.*
> *Yes, make our efforts successful!"*
> (Psalm 90:17, NLT)

Discussion

1. Describe a time when God's favor brought joy to your life.

2. According to Proverbs 8:35, when we find wisdom favor follows. Why do you think this is?

3. Where does favor come from? How is it obtained?

4. When we experience a trial, what does favor look like?

5. Luke 2:51-52 tells us Jesus grew in four areas. What are they? How do we apply this truth to our lives?

Introspection

1. Do I recognize God's favor on my life, or do I like to think I did it by myself?

2. Am I a loyal and kind person?

3. When I am at a low point, do I get mad at God and people, or do I try to learn from the challenge?

Chapter Ten

Fellowship

"It is not the fact that we are united in common goals or purposes that makes us a community. Rather, it is the fact that we share a common life in Christ."

—Jerry Bridges

Koinonia is the anglicization of a Greek word that means "communion by intimate participation." This word was used frequently in the early days of the New Testament church to describe the relationship within the fellowship. *Koinonia* was what the early church felt when they broke bread and drank from the cup of Communion celebrating Christ's death, burial, and resurrection. It is a remembrance word. *"Remember me,"* Jesus said. *"Commune with me around the breaking of bread and the cup of wine."* That is *koinonia*—a word that identifies the community and fellowship that should exist in the body of Christ, the church on earth. *Koinonia* embraces community, communion, joint participation, sharing, and intimacy.

All the believers devoted themselves to the apostles' teaching, and to fellowship, and to sharing in meals (including the Lord's Supper), and to prayer. A deep sense of awe came over them all, and the apostles performed many miraculous signs and wonders. And all the believers met together in one place and shared everything they had. They sold their property and possessions and shared the money with those in need. They worshiped together at the Temple each day, met in homes for the Lord's Supper, and shared their meals with great joy and generosity—all the while praising God and enjoying the goodwill of all the people. And each day the Lord added to their fellowship those who were being saved. (Acts 2:42-47, NLT)

Fellowship is the common ground we can all enjoy. It reaches beyond doctrinal lines and aligns us as the body of Christ. The truth of God's Word is expressed in different ways without compromising its integrity. That's the beauty of God's grace. Learn to celebrate in fellowship with those followers of Christ who express their worship in different ways from your expression. Of course, I am not suggesting fellowship with the world's darkness and wickedness. The Bible is clear concerning this.

Don't team up with those who are unbelievers. How can righteousness be a partner with wickedness? How can light live with darkness? What harmony can there be between

Christ and the devil? How can a believer be a partner with an unbeliever? And what union can there be between God's temple and idols? For we are the temple of the living God. As God said: "I will live in them and walk among them. I will be their God, and they will be my people. Therefore, come out from among unbelievers, and separate yourselves from them, says the Lord. Don't touch their filthy things, and I will welcome you. And I will be your Father, and you will be my sons and daughters, says the Lord Almighty." (2 Corinthians 6:14-18, NLT)

"Learn to celebrate in fellowship with those followers of Christ who express their worship in different ways from your expression."

Let's get real here. Jesus became a friend to sinners—to his enemies—in order to win them to him. Many times we allow religion to build walls around us so that rather than showing others the joy of being a follower of Christ, we cause them to roll their eyes at our religious pride and run the other way as quickly as they can. As Christians, we share the same assignment Jesus lived out on earth; we are to become all things to all men in order that all may experience the love of Christ.

It is incredibly important to understand that "fellowship with darkness" and "loving those in darkness" as Christ loved us when we were in darkness are not the same thing. Paul instructs us to come out from among the nonbelievers, to part ways with theirs. He is not instructing us to remove ourselves from the world. Rather, he instructs us not to unify with them, but to remain consecrated from darkness while loving them as Christ loves them.

Fellowship (*koinonia*), is reserved for our brothers and sisters in Christ. However, through us, God's amazing love is still to be constantly poured out into a dark and hurting world.

While fellowship with those in Christ's body on earth is important, our most intimate fellowship should be reserved for our time with God. And this fellowship is realized as we practice our privilege of prayer.

> *When we pray, we receive the gift of God Himself. Prayer is communion with God. He wants us to know Him. As we grow in prayer we discover that prayer is more than simply asking God for things, a selfish means to an end. Prayer is not an attempt to force the hand of God, but an act of submission to Him, with the understanding that God's answers are wiser than our prayers. Prayer is to impress us with God more than it is to impress God with us, or our needs. If we never gain anything from prayer but the opportunity to commune with God, that should be sufficient. (C.S. Lewis)*

The ebb and flow of your life is directly linked to your personal prayer life. Circumstances around you will not always be positive and perfect, but your attitude toward them can remain positive, and your actions can be those of a mature believer.

Prayer changes us. Prayer is the primary artery through which life flows from the heart of God into the heart of the believer.

I encourage you to consider carefully the condition of your prayer life. A healthy prayer life doesn't happen accidentally; we must be intentional about it.

Prayer challenges us logically and theologically. It is common for all believers to wonder at times, *Does prayer accomplish anything?* Our minds are preoccupied with conflict so frequently that we tend to focus our prayer on problem-solving rather than simply being drawn into his presence for fellowship, where we can then express our concerns and needs.

According to Jesus, prayer definitely matters: *"Keep on asking, and you will receive what you ask for. Keep on seeking, and you will find. Keep on knocking, and the door will be opened to you. For everyone who asks, receives. Everyone who seeks, finds. And to everyone who knocks, the door will be opened"* (Matthew 7:7-8, NLT).

Here are three things that can help us cultivate an effective prayer life:

1. **Create space for prayer:** We can't create intimacy with God; we have to make room for it. Set aside a designated time for prayer. The Gospels tell us that Jesus liked to pray in the morning. Maybe that time will work for you. Get up early and dedicate that time to prayer. Start small, perhaps by giving five or ten minutes to the Lord. Once you get a handle on that, move to greater amounts of time. Praying throughout your day is more likely to happen when you are being

intentional about setting aside time specifically for prayer.

2. **Don't make praying the focus of your prayer:** Many of us sit down to pray, and our primary thought is, *I am now praying. Praying is good.* But focusing on the fact that you're praying is like trying to drive while looking at the windshield instead of looking through the windshield. In prayer, don't focus on the conversation you're having; focus on the person with whom you're having it.

3. **Don't give up:** If you're praying and your mind wanders, don't give up. Don't ignore the thoughts that come in. Many of us assume that pop-in thoughts are distractions, but what if these are the things God wants us to stop and pray about in the first place? Instead of giving up, offer even your distracted thoughts to God in prayer.

"We can't create intimacy with God; we have to make room for it. Set aside a designated time for prayer."

I encourage you to study the model prayer of Jesus. It is, in fact, the answer to the great yearning of his disciples, *"Lord, teach us to pray"* (Luke 11:1 NLT). Jesus responded: *"Pray like this: Our Father in heaven, may your name be kept holy. May your Kingdom come soon. May your will be done on earth, as it is in heaven. Give us today the food we need, and forgive us our sins, as we have forgiven those who sin against us. And don't let us yield to temptation, but rescue us from the evil one"* (Matthew 6:9-13, NLT).

Integrating consistent and focused prayer into our daily walk is so important. Prayer is the invitation we have been given to commune with the Lord through our thoughts, our words, and our actions.

Don't make prayer a task. Remember that it's a privilege. Prayer is the most intimate engagement you can have with God. He knows you, so there is no reason for you to attempt to be anything but yourself as you open your heart to commune with him through prayer.

When praying, listen closely for the voice of the Holy Spirit. He will speak to you. Prayer is not a monologue, you see, but a conversation between you and your Creator.

> *"When Elijah went up to the mountain and there was fire and wind, he was depressed. Then there was the still, small voice of God. In Hebrew, that word means 'a thin silence.' Whoa! That's what it's like caring for your soul—getting quiet enough to hear the thin silence of God."*
>
> —Mike Yaconelli

Discussion

1. Talk about the definition of *koinonia*. How is *koinonia* lived out in community?

2. How does religion cause us to break fellowship at times?

3. If *koinonia* is reserved for brothers and sisters in Christ, do we close ourselves off from the world around us? Why?

4. Fellowship with Christ is the most important time of growth. What do such times mean to you?

5. What is the place of prayer in the life of the believer?

Introspection

1. Am I active in *koinonia* with other brothers and sisters in Christ? How?

2. I will take time to think deeply about my prayer life. Is it healthy or do I pray primarily in moments of stress?

3. What does the Holy Spirit mean to me? Is he my closest friend?

In Conclusion

And so, dear brothers and sisters, I plead with you to give your bodies to God because of all he has done for you. Let them be a living and holy sacrifice—the kind he will find acceptable. This is truly the way to worship him. Don't copy the behavior and customs of this world, but let God transform you into a new person by changing the way you think. Then you will learn to know God's will for you, which is good and pleasing and perfect.

Because of the privilege and authority God has given me, I give each of you this warning: Don't think you are better than you really are. Be honest in your evaluation of yourselves, measuring yourselves by the faith God has given us. Just as our bodies have many parts and each part has a special function, so it is with Christ's body. We are many parts of one body, and we all belong to each other.

In his grace, God has given us different gifts for doing certain things well. So if God has given you the ability to prophesy, speak out with as much faith as God has given you. If your gift is serving others, serve them well. If you are a teacher, teach well. If your gift is to encourage others, be encouraging. If it is giving, give generously. If God has given you leadership ability, take the responsibility seriously. And if you have a gift for showing kindness to others, do it gladly.

Don't just pretend to love others. Really love them. Hate what is wrong. Hold tightly to what is good. Love each other with genuine affection, and take delight in honoring each other. Never be lazy, but work hard and serve the Lord enthusiastically. Rejoice in our confident hope. Be patient in trouble, and keep on praying. When God's people are in need, be ready to help them. Always be eager to practice hospitality.

Bless those who persecute you. Don't curse them; pray that God will bless them. Be happy with those who are happy, and weep with those who weep. Live in harmony with each other. Don't be too proud to enjoy the company of ordinary people. And don't think you know it all!

Never pay back evil with more evil. Do things in such a way that everyone can see you are honorable. Do all that you can to live in peace with everyone. Dear friends, never take revenge. Leave that to the righteous anger of God. For the Scriptures say, "I will take revenge; I will pay them back," says the Lord.

Instead, "If your enemies are hungry, feed them. If they are thirsty, give them something to drink. In doing this, you will heap burning coals of shame on their heads." Don't let evil conquer you, but conquer evil by doing good. (Romans 12:1-21, NLT)

So, there you have it—my simple way of highlighting some of the most important factors I believe will greatly enhance your life in Christ. This obviously is not all-inclusive, but perhaps it is enough to encourage you to go deeper into your own exploration of his Word.

I began by telling you, "Intentional obedience to the precepts and principles of the holy Scriptures bring honor to God, and as we offer honor to those with whom we come into contact, honor from God himself becomes our own reward."

So, whatever the gifts and talents God has given you, use them well! Partnering with him in the various areas of our callings provides us with opportunities and joys that far exceed our imagination. My life is filled with great joy as I partner with the Lord and attempt in all my ways to honor him. I don't regret saying, yes to the Master.

"Serve well, and enjoy the fruits of your faithfulness! Your future looks good!"

—Steve Dixon

My Prayer for You

I pray that God will grant you understanding of your current situation, discernment to know what is the next right thing to do, and the wisdom of the Holy Spirit to do it.

A Blessing

May the love of God and the grace of our Lord Jesus Christ and the sweet, fellowship of the Holy Spirit be with you now and forevermore. Amen.

CPSIA information can be obtained
at www.ICGtesting.com
Printed in the USA
FFOW05n0709140616